# Empowered By Disadvantages

2nd Edition

## CRITICAL THINKING & ACTION PLAN

Lisa Ward, Olivia Tishaee & Jamil Bey

**Empowered by Disadvantages**

Critical Thinking & Action Plan

Author: Lisa Ward

Co-Authors: Olivia Tishaee & Jamil Bey

Front cover image: Guillermo Quirindongo & Jamil Bey

Editor: FaLessia Booker, The Editing Expert

Book Layout: Lisa Ward & Jamil Bey

Book Set Up: Jazzy Kitty Publications



REVISED EDITION

ISBN: 978-1-7330302-2-9



Email the author at lisaatward@gmail.com or visit www.lisaatward.com.

Email the Y&AEBD Program at Lisa Ward lisaatward@gmail.com.

*Meet*

# LISA WARD

*And Her Team*

## OLIVIA TISHAEE & JAMIL BEY

Lisa didn't see it or understand that her gift of writing, music and storytelling was the key to her journey, because she was only in middle school. So being a special ed student and having some regular educational classes still made life in school hard at times until she found her voice to bridging that gap.

Lisa started to find a voice that made her feel normal, because she, the special ed kid, was being approached to speak at different schools and community centers by teachers, principals & community directors of after school programs. Lisa realized with help in finding your voice anything is reachable.

Lisa Ward, the best award author of Empowered by Disadvantages & Co Owner Olivia Tishaee of EBD PODCAST is now working on a program called Empowered by Disadvantage Youth Program. This program & Podcast is originated and inspired from the book Empowered by Disadvantages.

Lisa Ward, and her partners Olivia Tishaee & Jamil Bey reason for putting a program together like this, is to bridged the gap between the teachers and students within the educational system. You see our success, is because we have always been able to find that connection with the youth. We wouldn't be the mentors we are today if it wasn't for the journeys that we had our entire life.

Olivia Tishaee model, entrepreneur, mother and wife. She is fluent in sign language and helping all ages of people all over the region with her performance with Vessel of Praise. Olivia is all things fashion, love for the arts and creativity. She uses these different platforms to speak against violence and promote positivity amongst the future generation and that is why Empowered by Disadvantage Youth program is important to her.

Jamil Bey, who is another addition to the podcast panel and the Empowered by Disadvantage Youth program team, he risen from being a gang banger to a counselor, mentor and amongst other things. Making tests into testimonies has been what keeps the young ones in tune with him. He's been active with at-risk youth on multiple coasts since Tuskegee University where he maintained a triple major of Mathematics, Physics, and Aerospace Engineering.

Empowered by Disadvantage book, podcast and youth program is needed. The book is already making an impact. So, now it's time to use that same impact in our school system. We will never have a world without education, and why would we. But, if we can't understand one another, how can we truly build the future of the next generation. So, that is what Lisa, Olivia and Jamil is going to do for the education system. They are going to give the future generation the voices they have been missing.

IG: officiallisawardspeaks, IG: mrs.o_78,
IG:dokroc.avodgy.dokroc
Website: www.lisaatward.com

# Mission

Give the future generation the voices they have been missing, bridge the generational gap by bringing understanding through situational critical thinking exercises, and encourage dialogue that will give the older generation better ways relate to youth to teach them effectively.

# ACKNOWLEDGMENTS

**Lisa Ward:**

First, I must thank my Savior, Jesus Christ, for assigning this Journey, project, mentors, and team to me. I am blessed to be chosen to do this 2nd edition that was created to change the future generation to having residual wealth with a critical thinking mind set.

I also want to give my business manager/sister Frances a big thank you for always supporting me in everything I do. She is my rock for so many reasons. She is also the reason I stay grounded, and I wouldn't be the woman I am today if it wasn't for her standing by my side.

I never thought I could be the author of multiple books, so I must thank my family and friends, who always encourage me to never give up on me.

Thanks, also goes out to my sisters, Mary aka Divine Beauti & CEO Felita, we are not able to see or talk every day, but our sisterhood and love is unbreakable. To my children, grandchildren, godchildren, nieces, nephews, brothers, mother, and to my unconditional love of my life, I do this for you. You'll are the reasons I keep pushing to be all I can be.

To Dr. Tameka "Doc" Wright, (RIP), I wouldn't have started my journey as an author if it wasn't for you. Our last months, days and now years that have passed since you have been gone are hard and it will never be the same, but I will do all I can to keep your memory alive.

To Olivia and Jamil, I thank you'll for trusting your stories and personal journeys with me and Humble Doc Publishing. I thank you, Jamil for giving over two years of your life to the dreams that I thought only I could see. Thank you for believing in me and being willing to stand by me in things that others might not want to. I thank you for helping me change the world with our stories. I also thank you for being a brother, friend, and business partner. Olivia, we have been friends for seven years. There are no words for the friendship you have given to not only me but my family. I thank you for putting your trust in me when it comes to telling the world your story. I also thank you for seeing my vision of the gifts that God has giving to both of us and deciding to work with me to change the world to be a better place. I thank you for being my bestie and business partner.

KIP SHU, my fashion stylist, and friend, thank you for always making me look good and helping me with my dreams overall, you are always there when I need you and, for that, you will always be a part of my team.

Rollo Robertson, thank you for helping me. Thank you for my first book award. I also want to thank you for exposing my name to the world of film and putting me in a room of greatness.

To my parents, you gave me the gift of creation.

To my grandparents, you gave me the ability and the desire to want to help people.

To Amanda and Alina, thank you for standing by me.

To my team, there are no words for all you have done for me and with me. Also, I want to give a deep and special thank you to, Angel Mystique The Poet, Robin Brown, Françoise Campbell, BoB DeNiro, Kimani Jackson, G. Jurel Jones, Randy McMillian, Shayla Parries, Guillermo Quirindongo, Malliki Saddler (AKA DJ Kaotic), Red Spade, Ira Spencer, Cynthia Talley-Wells, Kelz Tango, Eric Zeeky El Gross, PC Beatz, Reggie Davis, Latoya Brat-Richards, Teasa Jefferson, My

God Sister Mo Johnson to the end of the earth and Ms. Yola I love you.

**Olivia Tishaee:**

First and foremost, I would like the thank my Lord and Savior, Jesus Christ; without Him, I would not be here to see this moment.

I would like to thank my mother; without the life-changing decision that she made, I would not have a story to tell.

I like to thank my sister Gail who has always been my support person no matter what. We are like Celia and Nettie; no one can come in between our bond.

To my brother Corey, he always said Sis, you have to write your story you have to dream big, well, this is just the beginning Bro.

Thank you to my grandma Bernie (rip) for the talks on life. I understand now.

My circle is very small, and I want to thank the ladies of my life. Bintu is my sister from another mother; she is my lifeline and I love you dearly.

Nicole (my Chica), my firecracker, you have and always will be my ride or die. I am the calm to your storm. Love you, my Chica.

Selim… only I can call you that.. you are my forever stalker with so much love to give. Don't ever change who you are. Kisses & Love.

Kayla my songbird… you already know… no sermon needed.

To Lisa and Jamil, I love you two so much for allowing me into the folds of your life and family this journey has been amazing. Let this journey continue.

To my husband Mark, I know I am a pain and work a nerve to the core. I want to thank you from the bottom of my heart for allowing me to stretch myself on a journey that was unfamiliar. Especially for sharing me with the world, I know how much of a strain it has been. Your wife, with deep love, "Liv."

To whom I call Poppa Charles, this man has step into a place in my life that my real father has never even thought of, hell my real father does not even know I am alive. Orin Charles did not think twice when it came to inviting me into the family. Because of him, I now know what it looks like to be a daddy's girl. Not only am I now a poppas girl, I gained two successful brothers Jermaine and Andre who are so easy to fall in love with and with the two of them I gained two sisters-in-law Robyn and Lauren, I can't thank you all enough for opening your hearts to me.

Mr. Mike & Mrs. Carolyn, these two what can I say when it comes to making me look the part, they are hands down amazing. I don't have to worry about what the outcome will be. If I want or need a unique look, they always have my back. We have come a long way and have so much more to do so let's continue allowing God to use us for his Glory and show the world what God looks like in the human form of art.

I want to dedicate this project to Momma Carole (SIP) you have always taking me into your heart and I never understood why. Maybe at the time, it was not for me to understand, but, because of you, I now look at life a little bit different and appreciate the little things, the joy of life, the peace of life, how to enjoy me a little bit more, and how to just flow with life no matter what or who. Thank you for this lesson, life is short, and we are not promised tomorrow so live everyday like it's your last, you never know when God may call on you.

Lastly, I like to thank my kids Damisi, Marquan, and Alexandra for always saying Mom, whatever makes you happy. Mommy loves you to the moon and back.

**Jamil Bey:**

Let's start with God first…it's so cliché. It's a given, my drive, my determination, my resilience, my steadfastness, and my modesty…thank you.

To my grandparents, especially my grandfather, "Do it right, or don't do it at all." You were my inspiration to be a solid Freemason. Rest in peace to my mother and my stepdad. You both believed in me and sacrificed so much for my betterment and well-being.

Mom, I gained your level-headedness and peace of mind. You knew how to stay on your square in turbulent times and were so many people's rock.

Woody, where do I start? You stepped in and held it down like a champ is supposed to. I miss you bruh. You understood me being a street scholar. You kept me from crashing out by educating my mother on how I needed to move. My formative years wouldn't have been the same without you.

Motivation, the source of inspiration, goes to my 2 sons, Elijah and Isaiah. Your hugs and smiles are my fuel for life itself. I understand what unconditional love means through you two. I just want to make you proud and show you that ANYTHING is possible because you're mine. Just set your mind to achieve it. I'm showing you that it can be done. Never forget…THINK BIG!!! I couldn't have had you without your mother. Whitney, thank you for being such a great mother. They have an awesome rock in you. We made some great kids to brag about.

Lastly, I have to thank my team, Lisa, and Olivia. We got an unforgettable movement manifested from like minds. I never thought it could be so easy to have extended family. You all make it so convenient to entrust and share the vulnerable side of me. I was able to let my guard down and simply be human and open. The love is felt. This is my public hug to you.

# DEDICATION

This book is dedicated to the loving memory of my sister Edie Ward 4/16/76-12/27/22. You are Forever in our Hearts!

# TABLE OF CONTENTS

# INTRODUCTION

*"God doesn't make mistakes."*

This is a cliché that seems overused, especially if someone is trying to minimize how an event impacted you. However, disadvantages can be properly processed. To accomplish this, the disadvantages must be accepted and explored to expose any lessons that can be learned from them: See what the lesson was, see what you can learn from the disadvantage, and how you can make it to your advantage, then use the knowledge to help someone else. You can't have a testimony without a "test," and you would be surprised by who notices you overcoming obstacles without you saying a single word to them. Teaching readers how to overcome obstacles is one of the main objectives of this book.

Also, this book is an instrument to bridge the gap between the young and old. Often, the difference between generations can cause a loss of understanding of what youth go through, and this action plan helps to magnify the voice of students. Seeing things from a different angle not only assists with empathy but can help with teaching, the reception of the lesson being taught and opens the lines of communication between the pupil and the teacher.

This project was made to broaden the horizons of logic. Why can't we see the glass as half full instead of half empty? This book can give the reader perspective to lighten the load on those rough days when it is difficult to see the advantage in hardships. In many cases, this can be a daily process for someone, and seeing the silver lining in the clouds will make each day easier to deal with.

Dr. Maxwell Maltz said, "21 days make a habit." Why not start now?

You're going to read some personal stories addressing a variety of obstacles that Lisa, Olivia, and Jamil have been through. Assess the disadvantages, resolve the problems, and state the advantages. To put emphasis on critical thinking, each chapter has questions designed to develop an action plan after dialogue in group settings.

Everyone on this team has experiences that we learned from. We were young at one time and had trials to get through. We had to make lemonade out of lemons. We had to battle ailments and health issues; some are still fighting. We still wake up some mornings and aren't feeling motivated, but we know that the day must go on because someone needs us or benefits from our determination. That's what makes us go so hard when times are challenging.

We pray that our message is truly a blessing to people who take the time to read it. We have gone years without knowing that our problems were our profit. So, you must open your eyes, and most of all your mind, to what is real. Once you do that, you will see that everything that life throws at you is not always a pitfall. The synonymous relationship between disadvantages and advantages will not only help you become the person you're supposed to be but could also help you save someone's life—maybe even your own!

## Reflect & Review

*After reading the introduction, answer both questions as honestly as possible.*

How did you feel after reading the introduction and why?

______________________________________________

______________________________________________

______________________________________________

______________________________________________

What do you think you're going to learn by reading this book?

______________________________________________

______________________________________________

______________________________________________

______________________________________________

**A Student's Voice:**

Write down two of your own questions for us to discuss.

______________________________________________

______________________________________________

______________________________________________

______________________________________________

______________________________________________

**A Teacher's Voice:**

Write down two of your own questions for us to discuss.

______________________________________________

______________________________________________

______________________________________________

______________________________________________

______________________________________________

## ***The Importance of Critical Thinking***

Critical thinking skills allow you to understand and address situations based on all available facts and information. Critical thinking is the act of analyzing facts to understand a problem or topic thoroughly. The critical thinking process typically includes steps such as collecting information and data, asking thoughtful questions, and analyzing possible solutions within your own personal life.

For example, if you are on a basketball team and need to resolve a conflict between two of your team members, you will use critical thinking to understand the nature of the conflict and what action should be taken to resolve the situation. So, you must consider alternative systems of thought as well as communicating effectively. We are hoping to bridge the gap between teachers and students with the tools that are inside this book. We are also going to show you how to use the 3 Cs of critical thinking throughout our storytelling. Once you have completed the reading as well as the exercises, the doorway of communication between the students and teachers should widen, giving a better understanding of each other. The 3Cs: **c**ritical, **c**reative, and **c**ollaborative thinking will help the students determine what to do with the knowledge they have at their fingertips, as well as looking at things more openly from not only their own perspective, but the teacher's as well. Critical thinking is learning to see your advantages within your disadvantages.

# CHAPTER 1

## Half My Story

I grew up with three brothers and five sisters but always felt different because I did not learn the same way they did. Things came very easily to them so I would stay to myself because that's what was easier for me. I had my good and bad days in school, but then third grade approached. I was nine years old, and reading was not something I did very well. Whenever my turn was coming up, I would quickly skim through the book to find the easiest part to read so people wouldn't laugh at me.

I made it all the way to the eighth grade, avoiding reading as much as I could. When my family asked if I had homework, I would say no, or that I had already done it. I have a very understanding family, so you would think my lack of reading wouldn't be a big deal, but it was to me. I wanted to be normal and like everyone else in my family, as well as in the world. I wouldn't allow myself to see the benefits that life had given to me.

All I saw were my drawbacks—maybe because I had a teacher tell me I would never be anything. It didn't help that the teacher was a White man. I had other teachers who were White that were very good to me, but sometimes it only takes one to break you for life. I was a kid that loved older people and never cared what color the person was.

One of my teachers, Ms. Green, insisted that I should enter a school district writing contest.

I kept saying to her, "No, I can't do that, Ms. Green."

And she would say to me, "Why not?"

I responded, "You know why. I can't read that well and you know I can't spell, so why would you make me do something I cannot do?"

"You can't do it because you don't want to," she suggested.

I started to cry, and she asked me, "Why are you crying?"

"Because you're my favorite teacher and you are trying to hurt me."

"Hurt you?" Clearly, she was surprised that I felt that way. "I would never do that. I am trying to teach you that you can achieve anything you want in life, but you must do two things. First, you must fight for the things you want. Second, if there is a wall in your way that you cannot knock down alone, then go get help to knock it down."

She sat there looking at me. I asked her if she was done talking to me and in return, she asked me, "Are you done with me?"

I had a look of confusion on my face. I challenged her, "If I do this, will you help me?"

Ms. Green said, "Yes, I will, but you are going to do the writing and research on the person you want the paper to be about."

I did as Ms. Green asked and she did help me get my paper done. What I thought would be something I would not like at all started to be something I enjoyed very much. I would work with Ms. Green during my lunch period and sometimes after school. It took me three months to write the paper.

I completed my paper the week it was due. I submitted my paper not feeling that great about winning the contest, but what I did walk away with was a love of storytelling and writing. Now, don't get me wrong; it was still hard to write. I needed a lot of help, which was a disadvantage for many years.

I still avoided a lot of things from time to time, but Ms. Green did one thing for me—she put a big hole in that wall that I had up in front of me. Once I had finished writing the paper, Ms. Green told me that I had the gift of storytelling, and if I put my mind to it, I could be a great writer one day.

For many years, I thought Ms. Green was just being nice to me. I didn't believe that I could be a writer of any kind. So, what happened the next month? I would have never imagined! The list of the people who won the (national!) contest was posted. My class, along with the whole school, was called down to the auditorium.

As they were calling the names, Ms. Green said, "It doesn't matter if you win or lose. All that matters is that I wanted you to learn that you can do anything. I also want you to know that because your learning is a disadvantage to you, it could also be an advantage to others. Please promise me you will always fight for what you want and always ask for help if you need it."

I said, "I promise."

The next thing I knew, my name was called, along with 10 other kids. I was the only kid in my school district/city who won the national writer's contest. No one could believe it! From that day on, I kept Ms. Green's words with me.

It may have taken me a long time to write my first book, but what I did learn from years of working with many people of all ages is that what we think is not always right. What I saw as a weakness and a disadvantage became my strength and advantage. Words are now my voice on paper, which I hope is a help to other people like me. If I just kept looking at what I couldn't do at the time, I would have never done that paper. If Ms. Green hadn't taken the time to push me and help me, I don't know where I would be. I let a lot of things in my life pass by because of my disability, but I also never gave up. I kept my eyes and ears open to learning new things, and for years I kept looking deep down inside myself until I found what I was good at.

Now, look at me. I am talking to you through this book. Those who know me may say, "Well, that is *your* life. *My* life was hard, and you can't even imagine walking in my shoes. I was in a home with no one to teach me anything." I have another story for you to read as well, so open your mind, ears, and eyes when you read the next story.

There was a girl who was half Black and half Chinese. She had parents who couldn't take care of her. At 16 years old and with nowhere to go, she met an older woman who became like a mother to her. However, no matter how much the woman showed the young girl love, the girl could never embrace the love this woman gave to her. She ran the streets doing all types of things that she was not proud of.

As she got older, she saw her life as a big mess that she didn't feel was worth living. She would stay with the older woman from time to time, but never long enough to feel at home. This young woman told herself that she was nothing, so why even try to be better? Before long, she was addicted to crack, which is one of the hardest drugs to ever break free from. Drug addiction is an obstacle for many women of color.

Now, this woman has been clean for over twenty years and is a Christian. The disadvantages that took place in her life gave her the advantage of saving her own children and grandchildren from following that same walk in life. She has won the biggest fight of them all; beating a drug addiction that normally takes the lives of so many people, especially Black people.

Today, she is a happy woman with kids who have Christ in their lives.

Sadly, two of her kids fell into addiction, but all the kids are hardworking and doing their best to do the right thing. You see, her kids saw her life of hardship as a lesson to not follow in their mother's footsteps. Some decided to change the generational direction of their mother. As time passed, the woman could look back and be proud of her children.

We all have a calling and a job to do in the Eyes of God. What our jobs may be is not always clear, but life is not a book of "dos" and "don'ts." We must study and learn from our stumbling blocks in life and see what the blessings are in those situations. Once we see them, we can take them and use them to better ourselves.

You might even save someone's life after what you have experienced and learned. How do I know if this is true? I am that sixteen-year-old girl's daughter who lived life with what I thought were many disadvantages. But I now know that they were not disadvantages. So, for you to understand, I want to show you my life through my eyes and ears.

My mother's life gave me the tools needed to help people like her, but I would need to help them during their teenage years before they'd fall into the wrong hands. My mother's disadvantages were my advantages. Don't get me wrong—I didn't see it like that in the beginning. What child wants a crack-addicted mother? But if I had to do it over again, I wouldn't change the experience. It is the journey that God planned for me.

## Reflect & Review

1. What was the biggest gift that Ms. Green gave to Lisa at the end?

2. What were Lisa's drawbacks?

3. Ms. Green said to Lisa, "I am trying to teach you that you can achieve anything you want in life, but you must do two things." What were those two things?

4. What was it that Lisa thought she would not like? What did she start to love?

   Do you feel the same or differently? Why?

5. Was Lisa's relationship with her mother an advantage or a disadvantage? Why?

6. Do you feel it would have made matters better if Mr. Scoot was Black?

**A Student's Voice:**

Write down two of your own questions for us to discuss.

______________________________________________

______________________________________________

______________________________________________

______________________________________________

______________________________________________

**A Teacher's Voice:**

Write down two of your own questions for us to discuss.

______________________________________________

______________________________________________

______________________________________________

______________________________________________

______________________________________________

# CHAPTER 2

## Success

One of the most popular questions I am asked by the youth is how they can find success like Drake, Chris Brown, Usher, Bow Wow, Mary Mary, or MC Lyte. I explain to them that success is different to many people and is misunderstood by many. So many people want to be successful but don't understand the pain and hard work that comes with it. There is no success without pain. Many people don't understand the downside that comes with being successful, things like not having the time needed to grieve the loss of a loved one. I have interviewed many artists, and some had to overcome the pain of being absent at the death of a loved one.

There was an artist who had a very hard life. He was homeless and did a lot of moving around. The love he had for his music and for his mother is what helped him get through being homeless. Because he was dealing with a life that was very hard, he developed a tough attitude that led him to trouble in school and getting into fights.

His mother decided to send him to live with his father. His father told him, "If you want to keep singing and doing this music thing, you better straighten up." He loved music so much that he got his act together because he knew his father wasn't playing. So, the young artist started working harder than he ever had. He got the chance to audition for one of those big shows on television like *The Voice*.

His mother was so very happy and proud; words couldn't express her happiness. The young man made it through the audition. But the young man's mother did not. You see, he lost his mother right at the time he was doing the show. That type of loss will break anyone. To him, that loss was one of the biggest disadvantages for him to deal with. If you were to ask him, it was certainly a struggle, but it made him a better person.

He believes that God doesn't make mistakes. So, to him, the hardship he endured when he lost his mother had become an advantage because everything he went through made him stronger and gave him more determination. He now sings with pain, desperation, and love. He makes people feel what he feels when he is singing. He can show the people those emotions because of the seeming disadvantage in his life that was more of an advantage.

It is very hard to see any good in death. But death was never supposed to be seen in the light of sadness. When people pass on, we are supposed to be celebrating the life that person had. But we all fall into our natural reaction of pain and sadness which is normal when you lose a loved one. What we need to remember is what comes after the passing of someone. That young artist has gone on to receive music awards, volunteered to help others who have cancer, and he feeds the hungry. He took his journey with his mother and turned it into something great for others. He remembers what it was like to not have anything for Christmas and not have anything to eat. Yes, the loss of his mother was hard, but he also knows that her loss is his biggest strength. She raised an amazing young man who knows how to push past the pain and see the light of that disadvantage. Being successful is hard on so many levels, like not being able to spend time to grieve with loved ones or missing your kid's birthdays or birth.

People like Michael Jackson and Usher, who became successful while young, have also had their share of disadvantages. Those disadvantages weren't all bad. They helped them become the great entertainers that they are for the world to see and become the fathers that their children can look up to. So, when you ask about being successful, you must understand that success is a journey of happiness *and* pain. If you are blessed to have it in any shape or form, then you will understand how to see the light in a difficult moment you might be experiencing. You must take the time to dissect that moment so you can come away with the lesson it was supposed to bring you. If you can do that, then your journey in life will be so much clearer and better when you're trying to find success.

## Reflect & Review

1. What happens when or if you can't get past your disadvantages?

2. When the young man was sent to live with his father, how do you think he became comfortable working in an uncontrollable zone?

3. After the loss of his mother, how do you think he was able to maintain his success and is success hard to hold on to?

4. Why is it that the music & entertainment world are always glorified when we speak of success?

5. His mother was so very happy and proud; words couldn't express her happiness. The young man made it through the audition. But the young man's mother did not. How do you think he was able to go on after that disadvantage?

6. If you were that same young man, would you have been able to continue and what was the advantage out of the whole story?

**A Student's Voice:**

Write down two of your own questions for us to discuss.

**A Teacher's Voice:**

Write down two of your own questions for us to discuss.

# CHAPTER 3

## Learning Disability

*Author's note: This was the most difficult chapter for me to write. I was diagnosed at a very early age with a learning disability. My family was only told that I had a problem with reading and writing and once I didn't pass the first grade, my family was advised that I needed to be placed in special education. To go through school in Special Education and not understand why I was put there was the toughest thing for me to deal with. Kids teased me every day; something like that can break anyone's self-esteem. It's even harder when you don't understand why you are different from everyone else. Often, I wonder why I couldn't read as well as my other classmates or why it was so challenging to keep up with what the teachers were saying.*

Dyslexia is caused by relying more on Broca's Area in the left frontal lobe of the cerebrum. So, the logical processing problem on the left side of the brain affects analytic thought, language, science, logic, and math. But the trouble is not with seeing language, but with manipulation of it. For example, dyslexic people need to break words into parts so they're able to decode, read, and understand them. People with dyslexia have trouble connecting the sounds that makeup words with letters that represent those sounds. The human brain was never designed to read and the ability to do so comes from the three parts of the brain responsible for sounding out unfamiliar words, recognizing familiar words by sight, and finally pronouncing the word.

Statistics show that thirty-five percent of high schoolers drop out because of a learning disability, 50 percent get involved with drugs and seventy percent become juvenile delinquents. These statistics exist because there is no real-world solution for people who struggle with learning disabilities.

Dyslexia is a hereditary learning disability, so if one of the parents has dyslexia, there is a 50% chance that their child will have dyslexia. As of 2011, dyslexia affects 15 to 20 percent of the world's population. One in five people typically have difficulty reading or interpreting words, letters, and other symbols; for example, a dyslexic person may confuse small words like at/to, said/and, or does/goes. They may reverse the letters d and b and read bog instead of dog. They may reverse words and read tip instead of pit or substitute words like house and home. However, it does not affect general intelligence. The symptoms of dyslexia include poor short-term memory, concentration, attention span, difficulties with organization and time management, and physical coordination, but the most well-known symptom is seeing words backward.

When I was in school, there weren't many people who truly understood the brain of a person with dyslexia. Today, researchers are using brain imaging to learn how it works with and without dyslexia. It's been discovered that if a dyslexic person can learn to enhance their brain activity, then they could possibly become better readers with that, researchers have also been studying the various strengths linked to dyslexia such as increased creativity. So, hope is out there for the development of more wonderful tools that can help people with dyslexia overcome their disabilities.

There is no cure for dyslexia, but there's help such as tutoring, speech therapy, and eye therapy is available. However, family support is vital to people who have a learning disability. The world is very hard on people like me, but there is hope every day. Two French scientists, Guy Ropars and

Albert le Floch, have discovered that dyslexia could be linked to a problem in the eye. While some researchers disagree with this finding, I personally have found this to be true because when eye therapy was introduced to me, it was a big help to me (along with all the other training I was doing to get better.)

How do eye spots confuse the brain? The Maxwell spot centroids in people without dyslexia are asymmetrical, which results in the person having a dominant eye—just like humans have a dominant hand. Having one dominant eye causes the brain to cancel out the mirror image shape. However, dyslexics have two dominant eyes, which give the person a superimposed vision. Their brain tries unsuccessfully to process two of the same overlaid images. This can cause the brain to display a mirrored effect on the page, making it difficult to decipher letters and words. The brain doesn't know which letters or words to cancel out.

The Lili for life's lamp works to combat this by producing "imperceptible lights and flashes" that negate the mirror effect. According to the Jan 6, 2022, issue of the online website Reviewed, the Lili Life lamp has helped nearly 80% of users. The lamp has adjustable settings to find the optimal lighting for each user's unique needs. The lamp is also suitable for travel as well. For more information, please visit www.liliforlife.com.

Often, dyslexia can occur with other learning disabilities, such as attention deficit hyperactivity disorder or ADHD. I was honored to meet with Kellen, who has ADHD. He told me that he felt as if he had a social superpower. This advantage turned him into a social butterfly, and it is also why he can be so personable. Conversely, ADHD can be difficult at times because it can have a negative impact on the mental health of those diagnosed with it. Symptoms such as memory loss, poor time management, and anxiety can arise. As a Black male, Kellen feels that having ADHD does make things more difficult because society already views Black males in a limited way. The mental health of Black males has not been taken seriously as it should be. He feels like it is harder as an adult, mainly because, as a child, he was not diagnosed with ADHD. Also, as a child, some of the behaviors that are a result of ADHD are already expected.

Kellen wasn't properly diagnosed until he was in his late twenties. By then, Kellen was already set in his ways. He didn't have a mental health issue to attach it to at that time because he didn't know he had ADHD. I asked him if he was concerned about passing ADHD down to his children. Kellen stated that he is not concerned about passing it down to his children because even if they were to have it, he would show them that it is manageable. He stated that, as their father, he could guide them through it. He would make sure to have them tested early in life. Remember, he feels that having ADHD is a superpower that will help his children develop social skills that are needed in today's world. The greatest advice that he would give to someone that is like him is to remember not to allow people to define who you are based on your mental health. Your mental health isn't who you are. It is easy for people to attach what they know (or believe they know) about ADHD and yet again put you in another box. Don't allow it. The positive side that Kellen has experienced with his ADHD is that intelligence and common sense come as second nature. Most things he is challenged with are not difficult to solve for him. He thinks that is because of his hyper-focus, which is another common symptom of ADHD.

Many people with dyslexia, ADHD, or other learning disabilities quickly become overwhelmed and it's easy to take it as a weakness. Most of the time, that feeling comes from how they are treated by the public. How is it possible for them to conduct themselves in what's considered to be a normal manner when co-workers, classmates, and even loved ones constantly remind them of their struggles? Usually, it's not done intentionally, but most times, they're blind to the harm they're causing. They speak to us in a demeaning fashion or overlook us for projects because they feel as though we're incapable of completing the task. If only they could walk in the shoes of a person with a learning disability for one day, their understanding and outlook would totally change.

One day, I was called into a meeting with parents who were totally against their son's placement in special education. This young man was the most disruptive student in the whole school. He was in the principal's office nearly every day and failed nearly every class. I believed his behavioral issues were a result of things not going so well at home and along with the issues he was having in school. When I first met him, we didn't get along at all, but as time went on, I was able to make enough of a connection with him that he would listen to me when he got in trouble in class. So, when I was asked to be a part of the meeting, I had no problem giving my input; in fact, I looked forward to it.

Once the principal gave his parents the option to either place their son in special education or be transferred to another school, they were so upset they said, "Give us the papers and we will be on our way!"

The principal replied, "before we do that, we would like Ms. Ward to speak to you because we feel what she has to share with you could be a great help in your decision."

I politely greeted them, "Hello, I am Ms. Ward and I work in the special education office. I understand your concerns, but I assure you that your perception of special education is totally off."

The mother angrily asked me, "What would you do if it were your son? Do you know how people would look at him? Do you have any idea how rough those classes will make his life?"

"Yes, I, too was a special education student from first grade to eighth grade. I was blessed to be completely out of special education once I got into high school. But if I had to go through it again personally, I would. Your son needs this so he can get the help he needs to get better, not only in school but most of all in life. Special education classes, in my opinion, are always better, no matter if you have a learning disability or not. I say that because the classes are smaller, and you can get more hands-on experience. You also don't feel rushed or out of place. You see, when you are in a normal class, the pressure that comes with that is overwhelming. Do you have any idea what it is like to have a room of people judging your every movement, laughing, teasing, and bullying you daily? Listen, I get it; it won't be easy and we're living in a very harsh world, but he's a bright kid. If you give him the support and tools that he needs his chances of success will go through the roof."

I know you love your son, but you don't understand the things we have to fight with. I am an adult now and I would not wish what I deal with daily on anyone, not even my enemy. I am always feeling like I must second guess myself or feel like what I am telling someone is not coming across the right way. I would ask myself if it were me or if it was the person I am talking to. Why can't they understand what I am trying to express? If that is not enough, what about if you are working at your job or doing a school paper and you hear the words you want to say or write down, but it doesn't come out the way you imagine them to. I would cry myself to sleep on many days. There was even a time when I wanted to take my own life because I had no idea why I was not able to read or do my schoolwork like everyone else. I would lie to my mother about me not having any homework because if she was to help me with it and I didn't get it correct after her telling me something over and over, she would hit me. So, I would lie about school. I know what he is feeling and what he is not telling you. Why do you think he is acting as he does in school? He does all these bad things to express his frustration of being misunderstood and not accepted."

"I had a teacher in this very school tell me I wouldn't be anything, that I wouldn't graduate or even go to college. That was one of my hardest days in special education because I wasn't sure if he was correct about me. The best day in special education was when my English teacher, Ms. Green, convinced me to enter a statewide writing contest that I ultimately won. If I had listened to that other teacher, I wouldn't be here now, I wouldn't have spoken at events, I wouldn't be the mentor I am today, and most of all I wouldn't have gotten a job working at the same school with that same teacher who must come to my office and deal with that same kid, who he told wouldn't be anything. Look at me now—I am in this meeting with you sharing my story.

I've talked to people of all ages and most of them felt as if their learning disability was a disadvantage. I know that is how you feel as well about your son. But take it from someone who was in special education, it is not a disadvantage, it's a necessary journey to help your son get to the next level of his life. It's a journey that pushes him to realize that what he has is not a disadvantage but an advantage of a journey he did not see. I've spoken at many events to show that with hard work and determination, anything is possible. I have also shown those who have treated people with learning disabilities that you shouldn't underestimate people with any type of learning disability.

Thirty-five percent of people who are dyslexic are entrepreneurs and forty percent of dyslexics are self-made millionaires! So, I ask you, how could a learning disability be a disadvantage when there are so many advantages to what many people like Albert Einstein, Whoopi Goldberg, Tom Cruise, Ervin "Magic" Johnson, Steven Spielberg, Steve Jobs, Tommy Hilfiger, Will Smith, Mohammed Ali, and Daymond John and I have contributed to the world and our youth? We could not have made the impact that we did if it wasn't for the journey we were given. So, I asked her not to hold him back from greatness, to give him the tools he needs to be the next millionaire. I know I said a mouthful, but the parents saw things my way afterward, and now that young man is flourishing.

## Reflect & Review

1. Thirty-five percent of people who are dyslexic are entrepreneurs and forty percent of dyslexics are self-made millionaires! If this is true, how could a learning disability be a disadvantage when there are so many advantages? What do you think and why?

2. After reading this chapter, do you look at special educational students differently and if so, how?

3. Many people with dyslexia, ADHD, or other learning disabilities quickly become overwhelmed and it's easy to take these disabilities as a weakness. Most of the time, that feeling of weakness comes from how they are treated by the public. How is it possible for them to conduct themselves in what's considered to be a normal manner when co-workers, classmates, and even loved ones constantly remind them of their struggles?

4. Often, people with learning disabilities are treated differently. Usually, it's not done intentionally by people, but most times, they're blind to the harm they're causing to the disabled person. What type of harm do you think is being done and why?

5. Kellen has ADHD, but he told Lisa that he felt as if he had a social superpower. Do you see how he could see his disadvantage that way?

6. Why was this chapter so hard for Lisa to write?

**A Student's Voice:**

Write down two of your own questions for us to discuss.

**A Teacher's Voice:**

Write down two of your own questions for us to discuss.

# CHAPTER 4

## Fatherlessness

Doc and I were at a high school event in September 2017, speaking about what is needed to be a recording artist today. After the event, there was a 28-year-old woman who asked to speak to Doc and me about her son.

We said, "Sure, have a seat. How can we help you, Ms. Spencer?"

She said, "Well, my friend told me you've made a great impact on her daughter Linda and that you might be able to do the same with my son.

I said, "Yes, Linda is a sweetheart. Are you friends with the family?"

She said, "Yes, I am."

I replied, "Well, tell us about your son and what is going on that you feel we could be of some help."

Doc said, "You look so familiar to me."

I interjected and said, "You're right Doc. Do you work at the hospital, Ms. Spencer?"

She said, "No, but I have been to a couple of your events. I really enjoyed your album release party. To see what you did for those young people was amazing to me. When my friend Tasha told me to talk to you, I thought it was a great idea. That is why I am here today."

I said, "First, Doc and I thank you for the kind words and appreciation for our work in the community." Doc asked Ms. Spencer to tell us about her son.

She said, "Well, his name is Michael. He is 15 years old, and his father is not in his life. There was a Father and Son basketball game last month and ever since then, Michael has not been the same. You see, Michael loves basketball and he is very good. There are many colleges interested in him already. So, of course, when the Father and Son game came around, everyone knew he would be there. That is when all the questions started about why he did not play. It seems as if all the questioning took him to a dark and unfamiliar place. That is when he started cutting classes and not helping around the house like he normally does. He has been staying away from us and more to himself. That is not my son and every time I ask him to talk to me, he says I wouldn't understand. One day, I was picking up his clothing off the floor in his room to wash it. As I was doing so, I saw his journal on his desk in his room, so I read it."

I looked at Doc and then I turned back to Ms. Spencer and asked, "What did it say?"

Ms. Spencer said, "It was a letter to his father, surprisingly asking him questions like why he didn't love him. What did he do so wrong to make him turn his back on him and me? Does he have any idea what it feels like to have something missing from your life? Why weren't you here in my life so we could be in the Father and Son basketball game?"

"Ok."

I stopped Ms. Spencer. She looked at me with a look of confusion and tears in her eyes. I explained to Ms. Spencer that we had a clear picture of what she and her son were dealing with. I told her that we might be of some help. I saw how painful it was for her to tell us what she came across in his journal. So, I didn't want to subject her to any more pain since we understood what he was dealing with. I also told her that we might have to tell her son that she read his journal.

"We will only bring that up if we can't make any breakthrough with him. But I am sure we will, Ms. Spencer. I will tell you that these feelings didn't come overnight. They were waiting for something to tip it over and that was the Father and Son Game."

This issue is not as uncommon as people might think. What Michael felt was not new and is normal. Being a fatherless child is an overwhelming thing for any person to deal with. When we come across a fatherless child, we really don't know the impact this child is dealing with from day to day. America is facing a fatherless crisis and most people have no idea how bad it really is. There are over 18 million children, which means more than 1 in 4 kids, who are living without fathers.

Also, according to U.S Census Bureau research, when a child is raised in a fatherless home, he or she can be affected in many ways. A daughter who is fatherless is more likely to be in an abusive and neglected relationship, become pregnant as a teenager, have behavioral problems, or abuse drugs and alcohol. Black boys are more likely to have behavioral problems that can land them in jail. They can end up doing drugs and alcohol or end up neglecting their relationships overall. Most of all, Black boys can end up repeating the same cycles with their children.

There are disadvantages that come with being fatherless: so many young people and their families are destroyed. Young men may feel as if they must become their mothers' protectors since their fathers are not only missing from their lives but also from their mothers.

Doc told Ms. Spencer, "Your son feels that if he opens up to you about his feelings on being fatherless, it will add pressure that you don't need. Your son loves you very much but is hurting as well. He is trying to deal with his pain and trying to do right by you."

Ms. Spencer responded, "I don't need him to protect me. I need to protect him."

I said, "Well, see that is the issue right there."

Ms. Spencer looked at me and said, "What do you mean, Lisa?"

"You both need to understand that you can't really protect each other from a journey that you must take. You can support each other, but the journey that was created for you is something you can't stop. But most of all, why would you want to? We are always able to see the bad in things. We hold on to the pain that comes with all things, most of all our disadvantages. Pain seems to be the hardest thing to let go of or see anything good in it. So, yes, I think we can be of help to Michael as well as you."

Ms. Spencer answered, "That is great that you can help my son, but I am lost. Help me, how?"

I said, "What is happening to your son is also happening to you as well, Ms. Spencer, in a different way. You don't see it. Michael is going to need all of us to help him to see the advantages that come from his disadvantages. If he is open, then we can be of great help to him, seeing his true purpose in life. You are taking the time to be a part of this, Ms. Spencer and that will also help you find your true journey as well. You will also learn things not only about your son but also yourself."

"This fatherless issue that your son Michael is facing is also your personal journey and disadvantage. We are going to help you dissect this disadvantage, piece by piece. In the end, you will walk away with an understanding of the advantage that comes out of this disadvantaged journey that you are on. So, when I asked you earlier why you would want to stop the journey that was created for you, it was for that reason."

"Life has many journeys, some good and some bad. But our journeys help us become the people we are today. We as people want to be upset and angry at the things that give us pain. We never want to stop and look at what we can learn or take from this pain that we are facing at that time. We don't want to see how a disadvantage can be a help to us in life overall. We as people must start opening our eyes and minds so we can get the real purpose of the disadvantage. If we stop and take the time, we will find the advantage. Once we find out what the advantage is, not only will we be helping ourselves, but we can then help others. But the real purpose is also to put you on that right journey that was already created for you."

We did have many meetings with Michael and his mother. Michael ended up doing fine. He is now helping other young people. He also now sees the advantage that comes from being fatherless. He is not angry anymore. He found that talking about his feelings did help him deal with them better. We don't see Michael and his mom as much as we used to, which is okay. He is on a better path of understanding that his pain wasn't there to break him, but to lead him to a newer life.

## Reflect & Review

1. It seems as if all the questioning took Mike to a dark and unfamiliar place. Have you ever been in that place?

2. We don't want to see how a disadvantage can be a help to us in life overall. What do you think Mike got out of his disadvantage of having a missing father?

3. This fatherless issue that her son Michael is facing could also be your personal journey and disadvantage. What do you think is the mother's journey and disadvantage in this story?

4. Ms. Spencer said, "It was a letter to his father, surprisingly, asking him questions like why he didn't love him. What did he do so wrong to make him turn his back on him and me?" Do you think it was a good idea for the mother to read Mike's letter to his father that was in his journal?

5. Do you think it's a good idea for teens to have a journal? Why or why not?

6. Do you think the Father and Son basketball game was a good thing for Mike and his mother? Why or why not?

**A Student's Voice:**

Write down two of your own questions for us to discuss.

**A Teacher's Voice:**

Write down two of your own questions for us to discuss.

# CHAPTER 5

## Motherless

When you think of the word "motherless," you have so many people saying things like, "How could she? I would have never left my child in the first place." Life has its way of making even the best mother do something that can sometimes come across as unforgivable, heartless, and even a disadvantage to one's life.

When you are young and realize that you are a motherless child, you feel all types of things inside. You are always wondering why your mother didn't love you or wondering what you could do to make the woman who gave you birth love you and be the mother you need. You start talking to God. You may not understand who He is, but you know people talk to Him when they need help.

For those who know who He is, the reaction may be different. They become angry with God in some cases. How could He allow this to take place? A child who is motherless might feel this would be a good time to ask God questions or have a one-on-one talk with Him. When you're young, you think that you're going to get the answers to your questions, and when there is no answer from God or even from the woman who gave birth to you, it hurts. All you might have (if you are lucky) are some pictures and an official paper that is called a birth certificate with a woman's name on it that you don't even know. You become angry with life and sometimes with yourself. There are also times when you wish that the woman who birthed you had an abortion. You feel this way because why would you want to be a child who is motherless? Kids who come from abandoned homes sometimes can see many bad things. The system is not always the best place for an unwanted kid to go, but our choices were taken from us when our mothers walked out the door to never return.

Yes, there are some great stories of kids being adopted. I am a big believer in good adoption facilities, but we can't be blindsided and think there aren't bad ones too. There are many horror stories as well. There are stories of kids being enslaved, beaten, raped, and even killed who were adopted or placed into foster care systems. One example is the Hart family, adoptive mothers who committed a murder-suicide while running from allegations of abuse and neglect, killing themselves and their six children. We need a better evaluation system for adoption facilities and foster care so these motherless kids can be safe and have a fighting chance for a wonderful life. Being a motherless child is very hard and can come across in a negative light. It is very hard to see the good in yourself when in your mind, your own mother didn't or couldn't see it. You can stay mad at the life you were handed, or you can take what your life has given you and see if there is anything good about being motherless.

There are times when we need to pick a path. But are we the ones picking it—or is it a journey that was given to us from the very beginning of our birth and we just can't see it yet? For example, take the story of Mary, who gave her children up because she didn't know how to be a mother at the time. No job, no education, and a drug addiction didn't help. All Mary knew was that she didn't want to put her kids in the foster care system as her mother had done with her. Mary couldn't understand it because her mother had other children and she made sure to place those kids with family members.

Mary is the only girl who was placed into the system, and she didn't understand why. She would ask herself if it was because she was the only girl who was Black that her mother had given birth to. After thinking about it for some time, she knew there had to be another reason that she couldn't get the full story from her mother. Mary's brothers were White, so their lives were better—no foster care for them.

Mary picked a path of sleeping with many men, looking for love. In her mind, it was love that she hadn't gotten since she was motherless. She was blessed to come across many women who wanted to fill that void, but Mary didn't know how to accept it on an everyday basis. When it became too much for her, she would run away and be missing for months. To Mary, her life was a disadvantage, with no light at the end of the tunnel.

She felt that hopelessness until she got older. Then she realized that the path she was on had prepared her to be a fighter and to help other kids or women like herself. She even became a mother to a motherless child who loved her deeply.

The point I wanted to show in this story is that Mary's difficulties in her young life helped her to be the woman and mother she is today, not only to that motherless child but to her own children and grandchildren.

Later, Mary got a second chance to be a mother to her own children after 30 years. Mary gets sad at times because she feels as if she failed them. Her life of disadvantages may have become her children's advantages, but they are also the strong women they are today because of her. There is always a reason for bad things that happen. Being in so much pain or so angry at the time makes it difficult to take the time to see the true purpose of it and what can be learned from it that might be a help, not only to ourselves but also to others.

## Reflect & Review

1. "I would have never left my child in the first place." Life has its way of making even the best mother do some things that can seem unforgivable, heartless, and even a disadvantage to one's life. What is your viewpoint on this topic?

2. There are stories of kids being enslaved, beaten, raped, and even killed that were adopted or placed into foster care systems. How do you feel about the kids who are hurt within the system?

3. What thoughts did you walk away with after reading "Motherless?"

4. When you are young and realize that you are a motherless child, you feel all types of things inside. What do you think some of those things are?

5. Do you see the positives and negatives of being put into the system or being adopted?

6. There are times when you may become angry with life and sometimes yourself. There are also times when you might wish that the woman who birthed you had an abortion. You feel this way because why would you want to be a child who is motherless? What is your perspective?

**A Student's Voice:**

Write down two of your own questions for us to discuss.

**A Teacher's Voice:**

Write down two of your own questions for us to discuss.

## How Many More Times?

*By Lisa Ward*

We, as Black people, can't buy freedom!

Our ancestor's slavery & deaths should've made us billionaires, but instead, we still have to protest today for mental and physical freedom.

You would think after President Obama was elected the first African American president that, we were going in the right direction, but it just took one election to send us back to a time where our ancestors were physically and mentally destroyed.

Our generation today is still fighting the same fight. How many more times do we have to be killed, destroyed, and disrespected before you, the United States of America, give us our equal rights that we deserve? How many more times do we have to be beaten, lynched, killed, and even ignored before America answers a Black person's cry?

It's OK…we're not going anywhere.

I know some wish we would. The one thing that hasn't been learned in all these years about Black culture is that we have determination and strength. Others see our skin color as a disadvantage, and we see it as an advantage. So, I just ask you how many more times. How many more people will die saying, "I can't breathe?" before you ANSWER our question? How many more times America; how many more times?

The clock is ticking,

tick tick tick tick!!!!!!!!

# CHAPTER 6

## Being Black

Being Black is still an everyday stereotype in 2022. I am in my late 40s and I wish I could say, as an African American, that it has gotten easier. In some cases, it has. People like our grandparents, Malcolm X, Dr. Martin Luther King Jr., Jesse Jackson, Rosa Parks, Al Sharpton, Michelle Obama, and former President Barack Obama, to name a few, have done so much for us as a community and country. However, I hope you know that they had to face many disadvantages.

Malcolm X saw his father killed. He grew up in a time when being Black was painful to so many. So, Malcolm saw being Black as a disadvantage in his younger days, and he did things to fit in with the same race that almost destroyed him. He gave his life up for us. All you might see is the struggle with limitations. But when Malcolm goes to jail, that is the beginning of his realization that his life is not a disadvantage. With some help, Malcolm learned to see the advantages that came from his hard journey. All the bad things that happened to Malcolm happened for a much greater reason. The events that took place led him to become one of our people's greatest leaders, a leader that gave and still does inspire hope, power, dreams, and faith. He showed us as a culture that we were smart, strong, and can do anything that we put our minds to. Malcolm showed us how to stand up for ourselves and our culture. He also showed us that all races are not bad. Malcolm showed us that Blacks as a culture need to work together and be united to make a change that can be everlasting. Malcolm X's life of disadvantage was not only his advantage but also America's advantage.

Dr. Martin Luther King, Jr. was a preacher who stood up for what was right. He did not know his life would take him down a road where he would be beaten and put in jail. He knew being Black was hard, but if he could take what he learned from the Good Book—The Bible—and show our people how to handle violence with non-violence, maybe he could make a difference. Dr. King took a disadvantaged course of being in jail and being beaten. He replaced those disadvantages with the advantages of prayer, meditation, and meetings so he could help his people. In time, Dr. Martin Luther King, Jr. did so many things for his people and his country. We are still standing strong as a nation based on one of his greatest speeches, "I Have a Dream."

With the great sacrifices of people like our great-grandparents, Malcolm X, Dr. Martin Luther King, Jr., Rev. Jesse Jackson, Rosa Parks, and Rev. Al Sharpton, we were blessed to see the first African American man, Barack Obama, become the 44th President of the United States. Mr. Obama's whole election campaign was the beginning of seeing all our culture's disadvantages become our great advantage. Former President Barack Obama was the best person for the job because he was biracial. He could understand Black and White issues and bring the truth to Dr. Martin Luther King Jr.'s words: "I have a dream that one day this nation will rise up and live out the true meaning of its creed: We hold these truths to be self-evident, that all men are created equal."

America's 44th Presidential election was the first time I saw people of all races come together as one for a better world. He was what America needed to bring unity that had been missing for many years. If we can't take the time to see the good that came from centuries of pain, then we just don't want to see it. Obama was a man who took time to look at things around him to see if he could find the answers or the reasons why those things could be happening. Since he was able to learn from bad situations, he looked at those disadvantages and dissected them piece by piece to find their advantages. He ran America for eight years and should be looked at as one of the best presidents ever to run this country with eyes that were truly open to humanity.

## Reflect & Review

1. How did the poem "How Many More Times" make you feel and what were the disadvantages and advantages within the poem?

   ______________________________________________

   ______________________________________________

   ______________________________________________

   ______________________________________________

2. How did Malcolm X transition his disadvantages into advantages?

   ______________________________________________

   ______________________________________________

   ______________________________________________

   ______________________________________________

3. Regarding Dr. Martin Luther King Jr., what were his advantages? How do you think they helped him overcome his challenges?

   ______________________________________________

   ______________________________________________

   ______________________________________________

   ______________________________________________

4. Can you think of any present-day or recent historical occurrences/events that can show the disadvantages of being Black and how could they become advantageous?

   ______________________________________________

   ______________________________________________

   ______________________________________________

   ______________________________________________

5. What made President Barack Obama able to overcome his disadvantages to become the 44$^{th}$ President of the United States?

   ______________________________________________

   ______________________________________________

   ______________________________________________

   ______________________________________________

**A Student's Voice:**

Write down two of your own questions for us to discuss.

**A Teacher's Voice:**

Write down two of your own questions for us to discuss.

# CHAPTER 7

## Peer Pressure

Wanting acceptance and fitting in is a lifelong battle to some extent. Whether it's getting a chance to get to hang with the cool kids at school or in the neighborhood to being a part of a sorority/fraternity or a business organization, age does not discriminate when it comes to the pressure to belong. Group association can occur in many varieties and magnitudes… positive and negative. I've been a part of many different types of groups throughout my life. I was a chameleon through my primary schooling years. I was in gifted classes, but I was accepted by the street crew. Now reflecting on those formative years, I can take accountability for impulsive decisions that greatly impacted my life.

A naive, barely 12-year-old navigating the world can experience some impactful things, especially when anticipating the new world of middle school. I just graduated elementary school, but I'm popular in my own right. I have an older crew of friends and family members that I regularly kick it with. We're together so much that we consider each other extended family, even if we aren't blood-related. Our parents also handled us as such, so there was an extra layer of trust from them as they watched us grow up together. In turn, we became a local crew that carried the same popularity. With us always together, the occurrences of peer pressure didn't seem as blatant or offensive due to our closeness and youthful resiliency, but things can change in an instant when you decide not to give in to the masses.

By this time, we have transformed from a local crew of youth to an active Crip gang, and I'm the 1st generation of the set…15 years old and we're all a part of the leadership and direction of the clique. It's Labor Day

1994, and the crew was hanging out at my older cousin's house for a cookout. As a street-oriented teen, I gave in to some of the negative elements, like occasionally drinking and smoking weed, but I didn't do it much because it really wasn't my thing. My whole crew except for one were all older than me. While we were at the party, I got a page from one of the newer members of the crew, T-Bone. I got him down with the crew because he showed me that he was solid and loyal.

I called him back. "Ay, T-Bone what's crackin,' homie? Are you still coming to the cookout?"

He jokingly replied, "Cuz, I had to handle some things with the parents. I know that I'm crazy late, but I'm on my way." We hung up, and I let the rest of the boys know that he was on his way.

Once T pulls up, everything turns up; some other folks show up to the party, the music becomes louder, and the energy follows suit. My homies see T-Bone before I do, and my cousin. D-Loc alerts me,

"Yo Cuz, Bone is here. He got something funny to tell you." I gave a nod and headed outside to the rest of the crew.

I get outside, and I'm greeted with a smile and a short story where a few are interjecting their approval to try to convince me to join in on the antics.

"Loco, you ain't gonna believe this. You know those two cats from the other hood that I'm cool with? Well, they want to hang, and I think that they want to get put on. I just talked to them, and they're ready to get picked up," exclaimed T-Bone.

The other homies know that they wouldn't fit in and want to just beat them up for the fun of it. I wasn't feeling it because they weren't a factor, and it wasn't even worth wasting time leaving the party to entertain While I'm weighing out the decision, the crew piled up in the car, and there was no room for me to fit, let alone the two potential victims for the beatdown.

I said, "I can't even fit in the car. How do you expect to get the two lames? I'm good, Cuz." I start to walk off.

At this point, the whole crew made jokes and are laughing and yelling out of the car. I'm hearing yells of, "You're scared! Get in the car!" and other curse words. I stood my ground and my opinion. They pull off, screeching the tires. I decided to leave the cookout because my vibe was in a whole different mood.

I hear a car zooming up behind me, so I turn around to make sure that I wasn't slippin'. It's the crew trying to sell me on this stupid idea one more time, but they try to use a calmer tactic to lure me in. My rebuttal stays the same, and they leave out with a cooler tone that kinda softens my anger towards them, but I'm still in my feelings. I head home just to lay low and clear my head. The following day, T-Bone called me and let me know that the two lames that they were going to see never got in the car. The beatdown never happened, and they came back and finished the cookout. The people and food were gone…just music and liquor were left.

After I saw how the crew acted so petty and switched up on me, I gave them some space. I was still affiliated with some other Crip hoods on the other side of town, so my Crippin didn't slow down, and I still represented my hood. A few weeks went by, and I got a call from Bone.

He greeted me, "Loco! What's crackin', homie? Where you been at? How's moms doing?"

"I'm straight, Cuz. I been around. I been kickin' it in Homewood lately.

You know my Crippin don't stop," I replied jokingly.

T-Bone then narrates how the homies were plotting to jump me and possibly worse because of what went down on Labor Day. He then exclaimed, "What do I look like setting up the same homie that put me on to the set? You can count me out on that, homie!"

This was pleasing to hear how he held me down, and I thanked him for his loyalty. I then explained, "If these cats were really about getting at me, they know where I live. I still walk through the hood with no problems. I keep mine on me, and they don't want these problems. I'm Lil Loco for a reason, Cuz. They didn't forget that. If I'm such a punk, how can I still hang in other treacherous hoods with NO problems? I'm ready for a DP if they can give me a reason for it. I never backed down from a fade or putting in work, so they can miss me with all that." He agreed and shared that he might step away due to this issue. We hung up the phone showing love and understanding. Me standing on my own decision to not partake in the antics of intoxicated people was a hard thing to swallow. I hated the feeling of losing a portion of my close friends. As a leader within my own right, I had to show my firmness and compassion when it came to my disassociation of my hood crew. I still had other friends, and I even regained some of those friends back. After reconnecting to those same members that I separated from, I realized that my respect was never questioned, and the love is still present to this day. Though it seemed like a disadvantage immediately following the events, the lasting impression of standing tall and being firm on my decisions carried as an advantage to not only me but it impacted T-Bone to move in a more progressive direction. Trailblazing isn't easy, but you affect more than yourself when you positively go against the grain.

## Reflect & Review

1. What did Jamil do to counteract the peer pressure?

2. Have you ever experienced a form of peer pressure? If so, what was it, and how did you address it?

3. Have you ever helped a friend overcome a moment of peer pressure? If so, how did you help?

4. How did Jamil's actions affect T-Bone?

5. What were the results of people applying peer pressure to Jamil?

6. What do you think would have happened if Jamil had given in to the pressure?

**A Student's Voice:**

Write down two of your own questions for us to discuss.

**A Teacher's Voice:**

Write down two of your own questions for us to discuss.

# CHAPTER 8

## Abandonment

When I was young, my mother gave me up to the system/state. I really did not think about it at all when I was being shifted around from home to home. Why did my mom not want to keep me? It was not until I became older that I semi-started to think about why. No one really gave good reasons for her decision. The reason that does stick out is very selfish on my mother's part. During high school, once I got back with my family, I used to wonder what life would have been like if she had decided to keep me. I came to the realization that I will never truly know. I was too young to understand that everything happens for a reason. So, I built up this wall and decided if I was not important enough to keep, then you or no one else would be allowed to take up space in my world. This is how I functioned for years. However, that may not have been the best way to handle life, but it worked for me. I was bitter and angry; there were questions I would ask but never got a straight yet honest response, at least not good enough to my standards.

I told myself when I have kids, they would know the history of both parents, and I would do my hardest to make sure they came first before anything. Did I make some mistakes while in the path of being a mother? Yes, I did. But the one mistake I would never make was giving up my children to the system and I kept that promise to myself. Life may not have been perfect, but my kids were with their parents whether it being myself or their father. Now I am older, I can look back without all the anger that I held toward my mother. Who knows how I would have turned out if I had stayed in her care? My past has made me the woman and mother that I am today, and I am very proud of myself for not giving up when I could have thrown the towel in many days. I was meant to walk the journey that I have walked. I am confident, strong, silly, headstrong, full of love, but I have my moments and that's ok. What I came to realize is that my mother did teach me a lesson in all this. She taught me how not to be as a woman, a mother, and a person overall. I am thankful; I may not be where I want to be, but I am grateful that I am still here to get it right and I saw what my advantages was with in my childhood of disadvantages.

## Reflect & Review

1. How else could Olivia have turned out if she didn't have to deal with the situation at hand?

2. How would you handle your mother abandoning you? What are the disadvantages and the advantages that you can see in the story?

3. Do you think anyone in the family knew the actual truth?

4. Did you think Olivia played chess or checkers within this story? Why?

5. Do you feel every journey has a good outcome or not? Why?

**A Student's Voice:**

Write down two of your own questions for us to discuss.

**A Teacher's Voice:**

Write down two of your own questions for us to discuss.

# CHAPTER 9

## Grief

Grieving is something that you can't avoid, and losing loved ones is inevitable. Grief, by definition, is simply deep sorrow, especially that caused by someone's death. Many people grieve in different ways. Some people isolate themselves, like me. While others need companionship and constant attention. I've even seen where some die of a broken heart from grieving over a period.

I experienced and was familiarized with death at a young age. Once I became active in the streets, I became callused to the feeling because gang banging has death all around you. I realized how badly the processing of death affects me changed over time when my mother passed in March 2020. My mother passed peacefully in her sleep from prolonged suffering from a cold poorly treated 10 years prior. She was in her favorite chair with a half of a glass of wine left and her favorite channel on the TV. It took me over two years to cry for her; I cried harder for the death of Nipsey Hussle the year prior. I somewhat jokingly shared that with a homie from the set when my mother passed, and he shared something so profound. The homie replied, "Ay Loc, we've got PTSD from our lifestyle as a youth, and you are more affected by the manner of the death than the death itself." Unfortunately, he was right on the money. Death had been so normalized in my mind that only the manor of it could touch a nerve, possibly…but that isn't even a guarantee. But enough about that, this story is about when I thought that I had it all figured out how to grieve, and the universe had a rude awakening for me.

2003 was a tough year regarding this topic. March of that year was one of the hardest working periods of my life. I was working full-time and interning full time. You got it right…no days off. I'm at my regular job, just going on my lunch break, which is technically dinner time. I got a call from my mother, and that was nothing unusual.

When I said hello, she uneasily spoke, "Hey son, are you able to talk? I just got off the phone with your dad."

Now, *that* was unusual. He doesn't call my mother for anything, and I wasn't in contact with him regularly either. Trying to probe what's going on, I replied, "Uhhh, yeah. What's up? Why did Dad call you? Is everything ok?"

She quickly said, "No, your dad called crying, yelling, 'THEY SHOT HIM! THEY TOOK MY BOY!' I hate to tell you this, but your brother was shot and killed this morning."

She started crying and tried to explain how she attempted to calm my dad down. I was hit with a mix of emotions. Time stopped, and as I'm processing the moment, I'm getting angrier, and I could feel my temperature rising. The first thing that I processed was why my dad referred to my brother, which was actually my stepbrother as if he was his only son.

Secondly, he had my number and knew that me and him had a great relationship. Why wouldn't he reach out to me directly? My brother and I shared a common bond that we were both Crips from different neighborhoods, but I was cool with his whole crew due to my dad living in the same hood. Then, demon time took over. I haven't been in the streets for years (I'm 23 now), but the desire for swift retaliation came back to me like I was a teenager.

I don't quite remember what my mother said for a brief period, but when

I got focused back on the conversation, I affirmed, "I'm ok. How's my stepmom? How are my sisters?"

My mom didn't have any answers. I told her that I had to call her back and hung up. I didn't make any calls when I hung up. I tried to get clarity through it all because I was so mad, I saw red!

I spent the whole night trying to calm down. I didn't even call my mom or dad. I concluded that I was going to wake up early the next morning and drive from Alabama to Pittsburgh. I'm putting in work when I get home! If I could ride for folks that weren't even family, I gotta do right by my bro!

I got up early like I planned and packed a light load of luggage. I left the house to go to the bank to pull out money for the trip. I can't have a paper trail of a debit card in Pittsburgh if I'm planning on killing. I attempted to take out $400, and the transaction failed.

I had over $1500 in my account the day prior. The bills were paid. What was going on? I tried $300 and the same thing. I checked my balance…$20!

I hadn't talked to my mom since the call the day prior. She took my money out of my account, so I couldn't make it home. I think my stepdad warned her of my past, and she did what she could to keep me from doing something stupid and impulsive. She then confirmed it when I called her at work an hour later. This gave me time to analyze how I'm going to deal with my brother being murdered. I had to work later that day, so I talked with my boss and volunteered for all the overtime that was available. I needed to keep my mind occupied and stay busy so I didn't dwell on the pain I'm feeling. I didn't even tell anyone at work because they would force me to talk about it. I did this routine for the next month or so until it was compartmentalized and put in the back of my mind.

Two months passed, and it was time for me to go back home for my birthday. My birthday is on a Friday this year, so I'm amped for partying that weekend. I got home on Wednesday. Things seem normal and my mom doesn't even bring up my brother's death. We're just happy to be together again. My stepdad and I kicked it hard the next day. We laughed at movies and went shooting pool. The day seems almost perfect. For the first time in a long time, I went to sleep with peace of mind.

My birthday was the next day, and I had plans to go to Kennywood, the area amusement park, and clubbing afterward. I reached out to all my peoples to turn the city out. I woke up earlier from the excitement of my birthday.

I walked out to the living room to see my stepdad crying. He's holding the phone in his hand like he just hung up. He shook his head and said, "Hey J, sit down man. Clayton was shot in the club this morning, and he didn't make it." He started crying again. He couldn't even talk, and the phone started ringing. He just handed me the phone and I answered it. My Uncle Nate was on the line and crying just as hard.

What a way to start off my birthday! My uncle finally gathers himself, "I'm so sorry that you have to deal with this on your birthday. I love you nephew. We got to get things together, so don't stop your plans for today. Enjoy your day…you hear me?" I responded, "Unc, I love you too. If you need me for anything, I will be by my phone." I then handed the phone to my stepdad. I felt disoriented and on autopilot the whole day. I just went through the motions, and the weight and sorrow increased for the following days. I missed my brother's funeral due to mom taking the money out of my account. I had to prepare for my cousin's funeral, and things seemed normal.

I'm more concerned about my stepdad, uncle, and cousins.

We got through the homegoing ceremony and head to the cemetery. I'm holding it together and we are walking back to my car. As soon as I opened my car door, I fell apart, crying uncontrollably, and I almost fainted. My stepdad ran over to me and held me up. My cousins grouped around me because they were still crying as well. I was letting it out from what I didn't address with my brother. I was hyperventilating and couldn't get it together. Eventually, I made it to the driver's seat, continuing to cry. I finally pulled it in. I popped a blood vessel in my eye and had a headache for a day.

Reflecting on what I went through, I realized that I couldn't avoid dealing with suppressed emotions. Grief reared its ugly head months later. I was thrown into the grieving process for two people at one time. My body was uncontrollable and responded to the stresses in its own way. You have to allow yourself to receive and process the pain. My family, in sorrow, also felt helped by seeing my grief, because we're coping at the same time. In turn, it brought us closer and kept us consistent with staying in touch. We laughed as we shared memories and family stories to celebrate the deceased. Our family has progressed and become stronger due to these losses. That's the advantage and silver lining.

## Reflect & Review

1. What could Jamil have done differently when handling his brother's death?

2. What feelings did Jamil feel through the initial notification of his brother's death?

3. Who was your closest loss, and how did you deal with it?

4. When Jamil's cousin was killed, how did his body respond?

5. Have you helped a loved one grieve? If so, what did you do?

6. What were some of the positives that came out of the cousin's death?

**A Student's Voice:**

Write down two of your own questions for us to discuss.

**A Teacher's Voice:**

Write down two of your own questions for us to discuss.

# CHAPTER 10

## Voiceless

Life happens every day; the question is, how does one handle daily life? It was hard for me. When I was a child, I did not handle daily life well at all. I was hurt very badly as a kid daily. I was that kid that, you might say, fell between the cracks of the system. One day, they were checking on me and the next, they weren't. Once I realized that no one was coming, I started cutting my wrists because the pain and hurt wouldn't stop. I even thought about getting rid of my pain creators so much that I stood over them a few times while they were not moving with the knife in my hand, contemplating whether I should end it once and for all. In my eyes, there was no other option; either I would die, or they were going to die. One of the three of us had to go indefinitely.

I did not really want to die; I just wanted the pain and hurt to stop. However, I overcame those thoughts for one reason: I had little people to protect. If I went away, who would care and protect them from the hurt and pain I was trying so hard to get away from? So, I endured the trauma to keep my siblings protected. It took a while before the relief door opened, but it did open. Those were some of my disadvantages. I am so very thankful that I did not make such a rash decision and saw the advantage because if I didn't, I would not be here telling you my side of the story or helping someone else with theirs.

The second advantage for me was a judge at a hearing that I had to attend. If it had not been for her caring the way she did, who knows what may have happened to me. See, there was a bigger picture for my life and that was to be able to stand in front of you today and share my personal disadvantage with you so I can help you redirect your journey of a more positive outcome. Life is hard at times, but keep in mind that no matter what you may be going through, there is always a light at the end of the tunnel. Just hold on and never give in to your disadvantages. There is a calling over your life and you must be strong enough to see what that calling is, but for now, we'll just call it finding your advantages within your disadvantages.

## Reflect & Review

1. Based on what you just read, what was the hurt & pain Olivia may have been going through?

2. Would you recommend any type of counseling to overcome Olivia's trauma and why?

3. How did Olivia turn around from wanting personal revenge?

4. How do you think Olivia dealt with her life mentally and emotionally?

5. How do you think Olivia overcame the shame that she had to endure due to her trauma?

6. What were the disadvantages and the advantages you saw from reading this story?

**A Student's Voice:**

Write down two of your own questions for us to discuss.

**A Teacher's Voice:**

Write down two of your own questions for us to discuss.

# CHAPTER 11

## Illnesses

There are moments in our lives or in our family's lives when we are faced with the hardship of an illness that is chronic. You see, illness is something that we can't get past. Did you know one out of every three individuals has a chronic illness? There are many people who ask me, "How do you know if you have a chronic condition?" First, you must see a doctor to analyze any condition. A chronic illness is an illness that lasts three months or more. If your chronic illness is endometriosis, that is a condition that has many strange symptoms. The symptoms make you start to ask yourself whether tomorrow is promised to you. It's a condition that turns your life upside down.

There was a mother who, at the age of 30, was faced with the condition of endometriosis. She had heard of the condition for about 10 years but never thought she would be faced with an illness that would destroy her internally. She was okay with the condition that would make it hard to have children because she already had three kids. All she wanted was the pain to go away and the bleeding to stop forever.

She was fine with having a hysterectomy. Most women are not happy about getting their reproductive systems removed. But, since she already had three kids, that was a no-brainer. She was so happy. She told the doctor to take it all. "I will be happy to have no more periods. So, the answer is YES." I know at this point you are wondering why the person's name has not been mentioned, and that is because it is a story of many women. I'll give her the name Ms. Condition. All Ms. Condition wanted was the pain that her many cysts were causing to be removed. These cysts caused her to miss many days of work. She felt like she was pregnant and wondered if it was possible that she could be pregnant.

The symptoms associated with endometriosis are overwhelming for any woman on a daily or monthly basis. This is a condition you wouldn't want to wish on your worst enemy! We must start looking at other options that will help us get through these types of illnesses. For example, we can use group intelligence: doing things that can help a person with an illness feel better. Here is an example of someone using group intelligence.

There was a woman named Crystal who was given the news that she had Stage 3 cancer and she was a book author. After getting the news of her condition, she knew she had to tell her publishing company and publicist of 10 years. She didn't know how they would handle it. After setting up the meeting, she still had the support of the publishing company. They wanted her to get better and they told Crystal that she wouldn't want for anything because they would cover her medical expenses.

"Just get better," they told her.

After that, her publicist's reaction was very surprising not only to her but to everyone in the room. You see, Crystal and her publicist were friends. She relocated her publicist after getting picked up by her publishing company. They had worked together for 10 years as well. They did everything together. Crystal was the godmother to her child. She told Crystal she was very sorry and worried about her. She asked Crystal many questions, such as, "What is your recovery time after you go through chemo?" and "How long would it be before you get back to work?"

At first, Crystal thought she was asking out of concern and friendship. But that wasn't the case—she was asking because she wanted to know how long it would be before Crystal could go back to work. You see, Crystal had tour dates and appearances that had to be canceled, which meant no income for her publicist.

On that day, she walked out on Crystal, saying, “I am so sorry, but I must quit. I also don’t want to see what you are going to become.”

Crystal, with tears in her eyes, asked, “What do you mean?”

“You are never going to write again and if you do, you’re not going to be the same. I see what cancer has done to people and I can’t stay around for that. Goodbye,” said the publicist.

So, which one do you think had illness intelligence? If you picked the first one, you would be correct. Crystal started to think that her life was over after her closest friend walked out on her. She started to think negatively, but her publisher helped her by asking, “Who are you? What have you been doing for the last 10 years?”

Crystal had a look of confusion as the publisher continued. “You are a writer, a person who has written and spoken to many people. You have been encouraging so many people, so why would you stop now?”

The publisher asked Crystal another question. “Do you remember the movie, *The Five Heartbeats*?”

She said, “Yes, what about it?”

“Do you remember the part when Duck found out his brother and fiancée was cheating on him?”

Crystal was confused.

“Well, I will help you remember. Duck was giving his award acceptance speech. In that speech, he stated to the audience that he was told by his mentor that you become a great writer when you suffer more. Duck repeats the statement again, 'when you suffer more.' Duck states that he didn't understand at first, but he does now. He then thanks his brother and fiancée, who were cheating on him with each other. So, pain is not about pain but what you get from that pain."

As you see, when it came to Duck, his pain, which was at the time a disadvantage in his mind, was an advantage because, with that pain, he became a great writer.

There are so many people with chronic illnesses who might feel as if God is punishing them. But we must remember there is no happiness without sadness. We have people who have become motivational speakers about their illnesses. They have decided not to let their illnesses stop them. They have finally realized their illness is a sad thing but not a total disadvantage.

If your journey is a journey of illness, did you ever ask yourself, why you? You were chosen because God knew he picked the right person to endure the journey of illness. God also knew that you would be able to help someone else who might not be as strong. You must understand that dealing with any illness on an everyday basis is very hard, but you can end up helping other people or by speaking at events. Your ability to fight back with an illness is the biggest advantage that a person needs.

## Reflect & Review

1. There are moments in our lives or in our family's lives when we are faced with the hardship of an illness that is chronic. Have you or a friend ever had to deal with this, and if so, how did you handle it?

______________________________________________
______________________________________________
______________________________________________
______________________________________________

2. If your journey is a journey of illness, did you ever ask yourself, why you?

______________________________________________
______________________________________________
______________________________________________
______________________________________________

3. Crystal started to think that her life was over after her closest friend walked out on her. She started to think negatively. If you were her friend, what would you have done?

______________________________________________
______________________________________________
______________________________________________
______________________________________________

4. How do you keep going once you know you have an illness that is chronic?

______________________________________________
______________________________________________
______________________________________________
______________________________________________

5. Are there any advantages in this story? If so, what are they?

______________________________________________
______________________________________________
______________________________________________
______________________________________

6. What are the disadvantages within this story and what advice would you give the person that is positive?

______________________________________________
______________________________________________
______________________________________________
______________________________________________

**A Student's Voice:**

Write down two of your own questions for us to discuss.

**A Teacher's Voice:**

Write down two of your own questions for us to discuss.

# CHAPTER 12

## Endometriosis

Thanks to an amazing friend, I've learned even more about Endometriosis which is also known as Endo. We all know someone that has this devastating disease. This disease starts the moment that womanhood begins within us. You would think that the most amazing day of a young woman's life would be knowing that one day she would have the honor of being a mother one day and knowing that it is an amazing feeling. But there are so many women that are not so lucky to end up with knowing what it feels like to give birth. Women with endo are often ignored when they tell people the symptoms that come with it. We are told to suck it up or stop being a drama queen, not knowing that the pain is so bad that it is as if you are in labor every day of your life or worse. I was diagnosed at the age of 20 and I started my menstrual cycle at the age of 12. At that time, I remember my doctor asking me if I had ever heard of this condition. I told him no. He informed me that it was something that the medical field had just really started to learn more about this condition. The only way to confirm it is through a surgical procedure. I was 30 years of age when I had a hysterectomy, but due to the lack of knowledge of this disease, what should have been one surgery ended up being eight. My insides are so messed up due to severe scar tissue that doctors are scared to touch me; now that is funny. I was told that if I was to ever have to deal with appendicitis, I would end up in the ICU unit for sure.

Olivia suffered for years with the worst periods you could think of, especially after she had her third child. Her bleeding was so heavy that she would have to put on overnight pads all the time and change them every two or three hours. The cramping did not help matters either; she would be in so much pain that it would hurt to walk. At the slightest sneeze, blood would just pour out of her. She used every birth control available to try and control her bleeding and nothing worked. What took the cake was when she bled heavily for 72 days straight! She went back to her doctor and asked to have a hysterectomy. Olivia knew she did not want any more kids, so she was OK with having her parts ripped out. In February 2018, she had a laparoscopic hysterectomy with extensive lysis of adhesions and cystoscopy procedure was performed. During the procedure, her doctor found endometriosis, but this was not discovered until she was on the operation table. She is thankful that it was found, but she suffered with a lot of pain and bleeding for years before it was found. Olivia just wishes she could have avoided some of the painful trauma. On the bright side, she no longer gets a menstrual cycle and she absolutely does not miss it at all!

Our friend Jennifer had a partial hysterectomy and is still in severe pain. Some days, she can't even get out the bed or go to work. She cries when she has to miss out on things with her sons, family, and friends. She wonders why these things are still taking place after surgery. If you have severe pain like Jennifer did without a period, it could be due to inflammation and scarring caused by endometriosis that has been left untreated or unfound. Now we have a better understanding that this disease has so many harmful factors to us as women. The longer you wait to see a healthcare provider, the more damage is happening to your body. If someone tells you that your bad cramps are normal, don't believe them. You should ask your doctor if it is possible that you could have endometriosis. Please do not be one of the victims that, on average, take six to 10 years to be diagnosed with this condition. If you are a mother of daughters or caretaker of young women or teens, be aware of these common symptoms: chronic central pelvic pain, painful periods, pain during sexual intercourse deep within the pelvis, painful urination or bowel movements during their period, abnormal bleeding, diarrhea, constipation, or nausea. One of the most difficult symptoms to cope with is infertility which affects just about 40% to 50% of women due to endo. When it comes to endo, you may have bad cramps that will not go away with birth control pills or anti-inflammatory medications. Please understand that people with bad cramps does not always mean you have endometriosis and not all people with endo have bad cramps, but it is certainly something you should talk to your healthcare provider about if you have any of these symptoms I mentioned above.

If you are a woman who has endo, understand that this condition affects the entire body. We have learned that endo is linked to a higher stroke risk, according to the NIH-Funded Study posted on August 25, 2022, by the Endo Center.

Patients with endometriosis are nearly four times as likely to develop rheumatoid arthritis (RA) than those without endometriosis, according to a study in *The Journal of Women's Health* posted on Feb 17, 2022. I was diagnosed with RA about the age of 43 and it came out of nowhere.

If you would like to learn more about how endo has affected women throughout the world, please look at the links below. You can find more information by typing "endometriosis" in the search bar. We wrote this chapter so that the voices of women and young women are not swept under the rug. The more of us that speak out or write about this troublesome disease, the more pressure there will be to find a cure.

https://youtu.be/_s0lycRz_gs

https://youtu.be/85is8LGVZXM

https://youtu.be/zVL3DL8W_Ik

## Reflect & Review

1. Based on what you just read, how do you think Lisa handled learning about having Endo?

2. If this was you, would you recommend any type of counseling to overcome the trauma & why?

3. As a male reading this story, what is your viewpoint on what this disease does to females?

4. As a female, have you faced any of the symptoms that we talked about in this store?

5. At this time, we would like you to look up how many women in the United States are affected with endo?

6. As a male how does it make you feel to know your mother, sister or any female in your life might have this disease?

**A Student's Voice:**

Write down two of your own questions for us to discuss.

**A Teacher's Voice:**

Write down two of your own questions for us to discuss.

# CHAPTER 13

## Pain

Pain affects many people; it's the one thing we would take back if we could. The hardest thing to see is a child who is dealing with an illness that gives them constant pain. Who wants to see their child in pain? No one. When we look at what pain can do to people, it is heartbreaking.

I know you might be asking yourself how pain fits within this book. There is no advantage to pain, most people would say. All people can focus on is the hardship that pain brings upon them. Now, please don't misunderstand me. Pain can be overwhelming to many people, especially cancer patients, women with endometriosis, phantom limb pain, emotional pain, or childbirth. Pain is one thing that most people want to avoid, if possible, but it is also the one thing that every human being will experience in life.

There are many ways to look at what pain is and where it comes from. Pain is an unpleasant sensation, an emotional experience whose purpose is to allow the body to react to damage. We feel pain when a signal is sent through nerve fibers to the brain for interpretation. The experience of pain is different for everyone. Pain can be short-term, long-term, or emotional. Physical pain can stay in one place, or it can spread throughout the whole body. According to the Oxford Dictionary, pain is physical suffering or discomfort caused by illness or injury. To the brain, pain is a part of the body's defense mechanism. It warns us to act to prevent harm or further issues.

What I want people to do is to look at their pain in a different light than normal. I have mentioned that everyone has a path in life. On that path, there are good and bad times. The bad times are things that we must face, including pain. So, pain is another obstacle or hindrance that we need to dissect piece by piece. To do this, I need to take you on another journey.

This story is about a football player who has been playing since the age of six. He is now playing for the NFL and breaking all types of records. The young man grew up in the projects and his parents didn't have much. He was the first to go to college on a scholarship. His parents were so proud of him. When he first started in the league, he would come back to his old neighborhood youth center and speak. He would spend hours talking to the youth about staying out of trouble and keeping good grades. He would tell them, "The pain you feel from an empty stomach or from a beating you got from the school bully because you didn't have the latest clothing, OK, it's only a moment."

He would tell them to take that emotional pain and physical pain and let that pain encourage them to study harder. Anytime they felt emotional pain, to take that pain and make promises to themselves not to stay in that emotional place.

You see, that is what got him to the NFL. To many people, his pain was a disadvantage, but he used it as an advantage to make a better life for himself and his family. What he learned from his hardships is that there is no journey in life without disadvantages. Try not to get stuck in that dark place where disadvantage lingers. The point of any disadvantage is to grow from the pain that comes from it.

Another result of ongoing physical pain is that you grow to understand how pain can stop you from doing normal things like riding a bike, driving, going to the movies, or sitting in a chair. If you can no longer do those things, it gives you a higher respect for what a person can and can't do anymore. If you are a person with pain, you must think about the simplest things now. If you go on a trip with someone, you must plan everything out so it can be more of a joyful trip than an agonizing one. The advantage to having pain is being able to be more understanding and to show empathy to others, and that is the biggest advantage of them all.

## Reflect & Review

1. Based on what you just read, what did you get out of this chapter personally that you could use in your daily life?

2. What the football player learned from his hardships is that there is no journey in life without disadvantages. Do you agree or disagree and why?

3. An advantage of being healed from pain is that you can help someone who might not understand what a person in pain deals with daily. Do you look at pain differently now and if so, how?

4. Pain is another obstacle or hindrance. What pain are you dealing with?

5. If you were in pain, how would you deal with it and would you get help or not?

6. The football player would tell them to take that emotional pain and physical pain and let that pain encourage them to study harder. Anytime they felt emotional pain, to take that pain and make promises to themselves not to stay in that emotional place. Do you agree or disagree and why?

___

___

___

___

7. After reading this book and learning about Lisa, Olivia, and Jamil, how did their stories change the way you see people like them overall?

___

___

___

___

8. Were they able to change your viewpoint in any way or open your mind?

___

___

___

___

**A Student's Voice:**

Write down two of your own questions for us to discuss.

**A Teacher's Voice:**

Write down two of your own questions for us to discuss.

## References

British Dyslexia Association. "See dyslexia differently." (Feb 11, 2018). Retrieved from https://youtu.be/11r7CFlK2sc Exceptional Individuals.

"What is dyslexia - what is neurodivergence?" (May 25, 2018). Retrieved from https://www.youtube.com/watch?v=cuZ7uPa0fsY

FRANCE 24 English. "Science: is dyslexia linked to eye spots that confuse the brain?" (Feb 7, 2022). Retrieved from https://youtu.be/BMeMJpiz8mI

Holcombe, Madeline, and Augie Martin. (2019). "Jennifer Hart drove her six children to their deaths as her wife looked up how much they would suffer, a jury says | CNN. Retrieved from https://www.cnn.com/2019/04/06/us/hart-family-crash-inquest-searches/index.html

Le Floch, A., & Ropars, G. (2017). Left-right asymmetry of the Maxwell spot centroids in adults without and with dyslexia. Proceedings. *Biological sciences*, 284(1865), 20171380. https://doi.org/10.1098/rspb.2017.1380

Remarkable Minds. "Reading & the dyslexic brain." (April 12, 2022). Retrieved from https://www.youtube.com/watch?v=wUDZpmrZfz8

Sandman-Hurley, Kelli. "What is dyslexia?" (Jul 15, 2013). Retrieved from https://www.youtube.com/watch?v=zafiGBrFkRM

Schumacher, J., Hoffmann, P., Schmäl, C., Schulte-Körne, G., & Nöthen, M. M. (2007). Genetics of dyslexia: the evolving landscape. Journal of medical genetics, 44(5), 289–297. https://doi.org/10.1136/jmg.2006.046516

Skill Boosters. "What is Neurodiversity?" (Jun 27, 2022). Retrieved from https://youtu.be/GLGLLylcDvM

U.S. Census Bureau. "Living arrangements of children under 18 years old: 1960 to present." (2021). Washington, D.C.: U.S. Census Bureau. Retrieved from https://www.census.gov/programs-surveys/cps/data-detail.html

# ABOUT THE AUTHORS

**Lisa Ward** is a motivational speaker, published author, manager, artist developer, mentor and founder of Avodgy Collection, Humble Doc Publishing, SECDUM Magazine, and Deadline Production/management. Her book, Empowered by Disadvantages, chronicles her many adversities and how these have empowered and propelled her to the many successes in her life such as establishing a magazine that interviewed various famous & iconic artists. Lisa is also passionately dedicated to transforming today's youth into successful entertainers, entrepreneurs, and authors.

Ms. Ward gets her love for the entertainment industry, writing, and business hustle honestly from her mother, her business-savvy father, and her sisters. She is the second oldest sibling of nine creative and gifted children. She has accomplished a great deal in 40 years.

God changed Lisa's life and direction, transitioning her gifts toward impacting the youth of today. Lisa has always loved working with children and young adults. She has a strong desire to develop their careers and businesses while motivating others to view their hardships in a positive way. Keep your eyes on Lisa Ward and support her endeavors because whatever goal or project she has set her mind to, she is going to accomplish it and help as many people as she can!

**Olivia Tishaee**

Co-author Olivia Tishaee hails from Camden, New Jersey. As a model, wife, and mother of three, Olivia uses her character traits of being strong, loving, and hopeful to motivate others and speak life into everyone she encounters. Being a teenage mother did not stop her from achieving her goals. Mrs. Olivia is fluent in American sign language and a god-fearing woman whose passion is to touch the hearts of all those who are willing to accept love and to help others in whatever way she can.

Olivia is very involved with the Empowered by Disadvantages mission because she understands what it is like to be part of the foster care and adoption system. Like Jamil and Lisa, Olivia desires to be a voice for voiceless children; the EBD podcast and book allows her to accomplish this goal. Olivia positively impacts everyone that she meets. She reminds readers that you never know what someone may be going through, so please be careful about how you treat that person; you could be their last source of life. Further, we should always speak life because the tongue is a powerful weapon. Olivia chooses to use hers for good!

**Jamil Bey**

Jamil Bey was born May 23, 1979, in Pittsburgh, PA. From the age of 4, he was raised between there and Miami Beach, FL. He was always the youngest in his social circles, which caused him to grow up a little faster than his peers. At the age of 12, he became an active gangbanger; despite this, he still maintained a 3.9 GPA. Jamil received an academic scholarship to Tuskegee University where he triple majored in Mathematics, Physics, and Aerospace Engineering. While in college, he worked as an assistant teacher at Tuskegee Institute Middle School and tutored students from elementary through college. Jamil volunteered as a gang counselor in several cities and for the YMCA as an after-school counselor. This background is what led him to be such a great fit for the EBD team.

Jamil and Lisa met while working at the same job. They had so many things in common that they became business partners for the clothing line Avodgy. Lisa had already written Empowered by Disadvantages, beginning a movement that Jamil related to because of his past. When Lisa proposed that Jamil be added to the EBD Podcast panel, he jumped on the opportunity without a second thought!

Mr. Bey uses his street experience and youthful spirit to assist youth with overcoming adolescent challenges and disadvantages. His background in dealing with at-risk youth enables him to tap into and address underlying troubling issues. Often, when kids act out, something else triggers those attitudes, and Jamil is proficient in dissecting those issues to resolve gaps in communication gap and refocusing on learning. Mr. Bey's biggest accomplishment was seeing the "problem children" that he taught in middle school become high school honors students and giving him credit for enjoying school and getting good grades. These students would graduate and pursue higher education as if they never had a hiccup in their primary schooling! Lisa's team has the same priorities—to give the youth the voice they deserve, and Jamil has joined "ten toes down" as part of the movement.

Printed in the USA
CPSIA information can be obtained
at www.ICGtesting.com
LVHW011920010324
773178LV00013B/151